Numbers are keyed to captions throughout the book.

Numbers are keyed to captions throughout the book.

A Field Guide to Wildflowers Coloring Book

Roger Tory Peterson
and Frances Tenenbaum

*Illustrations by Roger Tory Peterson
and Virginia Savage*

Houghton Mifflin Company   Boston   New York

Copyright © 1982 by
Houghton Mifflin Company

For permission to reproduce selections
from this book, write to Permissions,
Houghton Mifflin Company,
215 Park Avenue South,
New York, New York 10003.

Library of Congress Cataloging
in Publication Data

Peterson, Roger Tory (date)
A field guide to wildflowers coloring
book.
1. Wildflowers—North America
—Pictorial Works. 2. Wildflowers
—North America—Identification.
3. Painting Books. I. Tenenbaum.
Frances. II. Title.
QK112.P47 1982 582.13'097
82-6253 AACR2
ISBN 0-395-32522-6 (pbk.)

Printed in the
United States of America

DPI 19 18 17 16 15 14 13

Introduction

Finding flowers, or "botanizing," is a visual activity; it trains the eye. Most beginners soon acquire *A Field Guide to Wildflowers* — a handy, pocket-sized book that is illustrated by my own drawings — or its companions, *A Field Guide to Pacific States Wildflowers* and *A Field Guide to Rocky Mountain Wildflowers*. These guides offer shortcuts to recognizing flowers, using little arrows that point to the special features by which one kind of flower may be known from another. Many of my line drawings are included in this coloring book.

Even a person who is colorblind can become skilled at identifying flowers by the arrangement of petals, leaf shapes, veins, and other structures; but for most of us color is the first step. This coloring book will sharpen your observations and condition your memory for the days you spend out-of-doors. By filling in the colors during evenings at home or on winter days before spring brings the world to life, you will be better informed about these same plants when you find them in bloom. You may even wish to color up your own Field Guide, as many people have done. But color alone is not enough to identify most flowers. Their colors do not fall into patterns as they do in birds. Every buttercup, for example, is yellow. You must also look at other details to narrow your flower down to a Swamp Buttercup, Early Buttercup, or whatever. Nevertheless, color is step number one.

There are literally thousands of species of wildflowers in North America. In this coloring book we can show only a few. Some of the most familiar flowers are those of the roadside that have escaped from gardens or were introduced from Europe.

A coloring book such as this will help your color perception, but will not teach you to draw unless you copy the basic line drawings. You might even try to sketch the flowers you find growing in the wild.

Finding flowers can be rewarding in many ways — but above all it sharpens the senses, especially the eye. If you draw or paint, the sense of touch also comes into play as you transfer the images of the eye and the mind by hand to paper. In searching for flowers and perhaps in drawing them, you also become more aware of the natural world — the real world.

Most of you may find colored pencils best suited for coloring this book, but if you are handy with brushes and paints, you may prefer to fill in the outlines with watercolors. Crayons, too, can be used. But don't labor, have fun. That is what this coloring book is all about.

Roger Tory Peterson

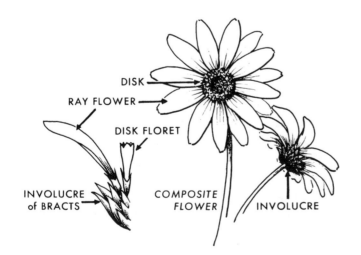

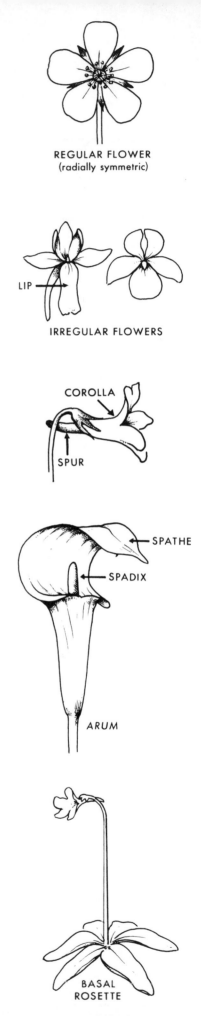

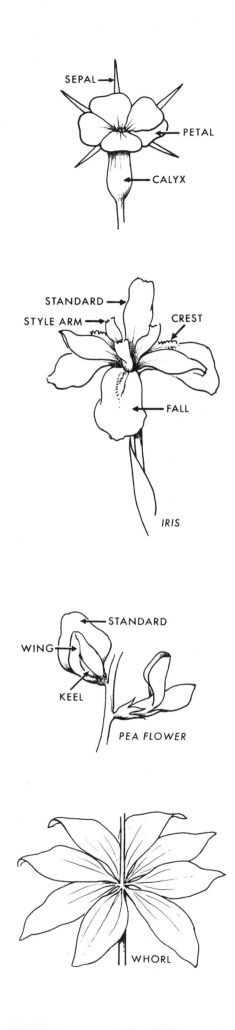

SEPAL → PETAL → CALYX

STANDARD → STYLE ARM → CREST → FALL

IRIS

STANDARD WING → KEEL

PEA FLOWER

WHORL

About This Book

For years, my daily comings and goings took me along a stretch of the Long Island Expressway, a road whose embankments usually presented a dismal vista of litter and weeds — except when covered with dingy snow! So one day when I found myself actually taking pleasure in that roadside, I wondered what had changed. Although the litter remained, what struck my eyes were black-eyed Susans, yellow coreopsis, sky-blue chicory, bright white daisies, and even a giant, grayish green mullein.

Of course the plants had not changed; the difference was in the eye of the beholder. Over the winter I had become interested in flower identification; now that I knew their names, what once were weeds had turned into wildflowers. And an ugly roadside had become a source of pleasure. One of the nice things about identifying wildflowers is that you can do it almost anywhere. The woodlands have their lady's-slippers, but the crack in a city pavement may be home to a scarlet pimpernel.

How to Use This Book

Arrangement. The flowers in this book are arranged by the places in which you are most likely to find them. We cover four basic habitats: woods, fields, wetlands, and sandy soil. But remember the words "most likely," because flowers do not always respect strict boundary lines. You may find a woodland flower in a field at the edge of the woods. You may even find one in a sunny marsh, where moisture will make up for the lack of shade. You would be most unlikely, however, to find a woodland flower in a *dry* sunny field. In cases where a flower commonly grows in more than one habitat, the caption will make a note of it.

Botanical terms. Since the purpose of this book is to teach flower identification, not botany, the parts of the flowers are generally described in familiar terms. Thus, if something looks like a petal it probably will be called a petal — even though technically it may be a *ray*, a *bract* (modified leaf), or a *sepal*. Sometimes you may find an unfamiliar word used to describe a part of the flower. If the term is not explained in the caption, you will find it in the pictorial glossary.

Coloring the drawings. You will get the best results with colored pencils. Crayons will work, but their larger points may make it harder to color the more delicate flower parts.

Occasionally — unfortunately, very occasionally — a flower color can be described as simply "red," "light blue," or even "bright yellow." The truth is that not many flowers come in simple, clear colors. More often than not, the directions will advise you to color the flower "whitish," "pinkish," "lavender-blue," or "purplish brown."

Don't worry too much about getting the colors exactly right. Whatever "pinkish" or any other color conjures up in your mind's eye is the color to try to achieve. Remember, too, that one person's orange is another one's red, and even the botanist who describes a flower as, say, reddish purple, is describing it in personal terms. Furthermore, a flower seen at noon on a sunny day will look slightly different in color than that same flower seen at dusk. All of the flowers are reproduced in color on the inside covers of the book; the numbers shown there are keyed to the numbers at the ends of the captions.

However you use this book, you will find it a pleasurable way to learn about wildflowers.

Frances Tenenbaum

Harbingers of Spring

Sometimes these woodland flowers bloom before the snow is off the ground. Perhaps because they are so early, all of these small plants have rather delicate coloring.

The **Round-leaved Yellow Violet** is one of the smaller violets. The yellow flowers stand from 2 to 5 inches above the woodland soil. (1)

The **Round-lobed Hepatica** has flowers of white, pink, lavender, or blue, with bushy whitish stamens in the center. The bracts (modified leaves) supporting the petals are green. (2) A plant with the same kind of flowers but pointed leaves is the Sharp-lobed Hepatica (not shown).

The pale green leaf of the **Bloodroot** is folded around the stem. The flower is pure white with a yellow center. (3)

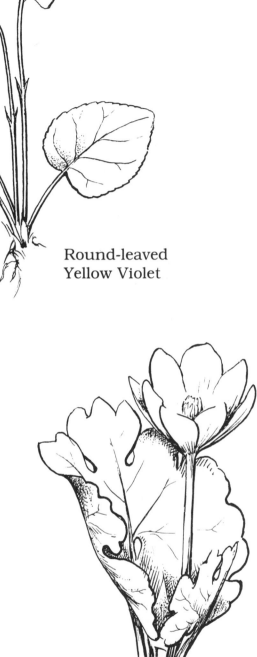

Round-leaved
Yellow Violet

Round-lobed
Hepatica

Bloodroot

Woods

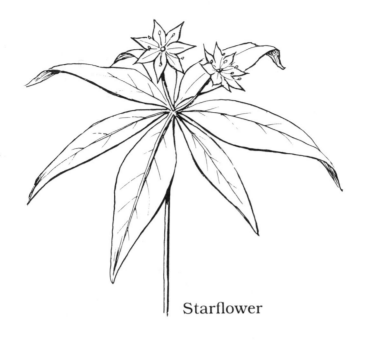

Starflower

Small Spring Flowers

The petals of the fragile white **Starflower** form a six- or seven-pointed star, which sits above a whorl of shiny bronze-green leaves. (4)

Anemones are also known as "windflowers" because their stems are so fragile that they flutter in the slightest breeze. The white petals of the **Wood Anemone** surround a center of yellow pistils and stamens. (5)

The cloverlike leaflets of the **Common Wood-sorrel** look like upside-down hearts. The flower petals are white or pink with darker pink veins. (6)

Common
Wood-sorrel

Wood Anemone

Wild Orchids

The wild orchids on this page are called "lady's-slippers" because of the shape of the lip petal. Does it remind you of a slipper or a pouch?

The large lip of the **Showy Lady's-slipper** is rose-colored at the top, shading to white at the edge. The three side petals are white. This is the largest of the northern wild orchids. It grows in swamps as well as in wet woods. (7)

The lip or pouch of the **Yellow Lady's-slipper** is yellow, and the side petals, which are twisted and narrow, are striped with brownish yellow. (8)

The **Moccasin-flower** is also called the Pink Lady's-slipper. The deeply cleft pouch is dark pink with red veins. The side petals are greenish brown. (9)

Woods

Showy
Lady's-slipper

Moccasin-flower

Yellow
Lady's-slipper

Woods

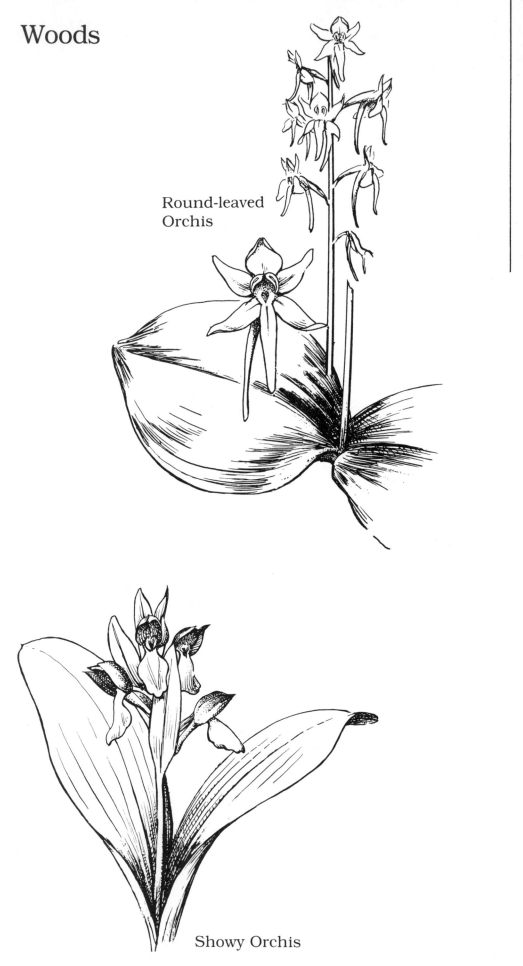

Round-leaved
Orchis

Showy Orchis

The long tapering lip and the even longer spur are typical of the **Round-leaved Orchis.** The flowers are greenish white. (10)

The lip of the **Small Round-leaved Orchis** is white spotted with magenta, and the other petals are white to mauve. (11)

The purple or rose hood of the **Showy Orchis** contrasts strikingly with the white lip below. (12)

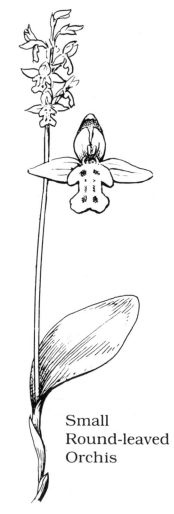

Small
Round-leaved
Orchis

Wild Orchids

The petals of the **Broad-lipped Twayblade** — including the broad, notched lip — are greenish yellow. The sepals are purplish. This twayblade also grows in swamps and damp soil. (13)

The strange long sepals of the **Whorled Pogonia** are reddish purple. The petals are greenish yellow, except for the lip, which is streaked with purple. (14)

The single large leaf of the **Puttyroot** develops in the summer, lasts over the winter, and withers before the flowers bloom. The blossoms are whitish, yellowish, or greenish. The crinkly-edged lip is marked with purple. (15)

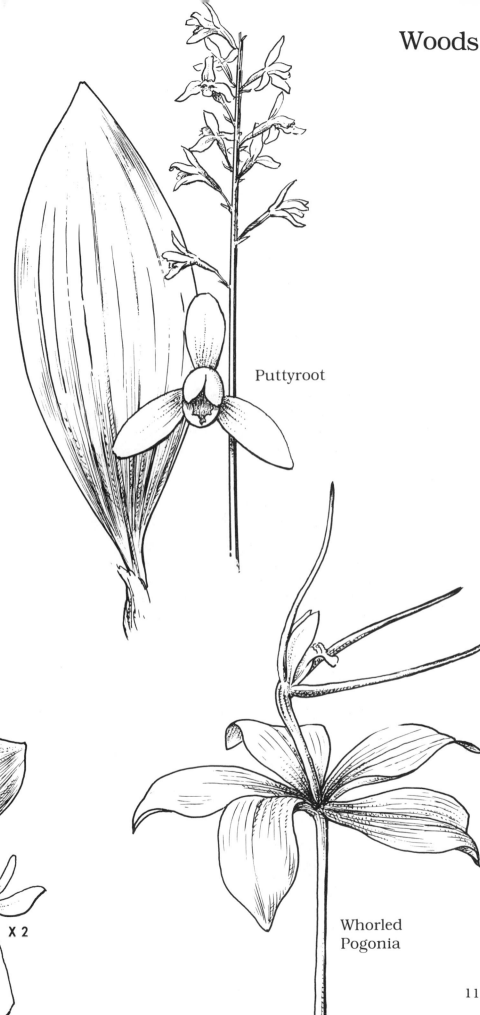

Puttyroot

Broad-lipped
Twayblade

X 2

Whorled
Pogonia

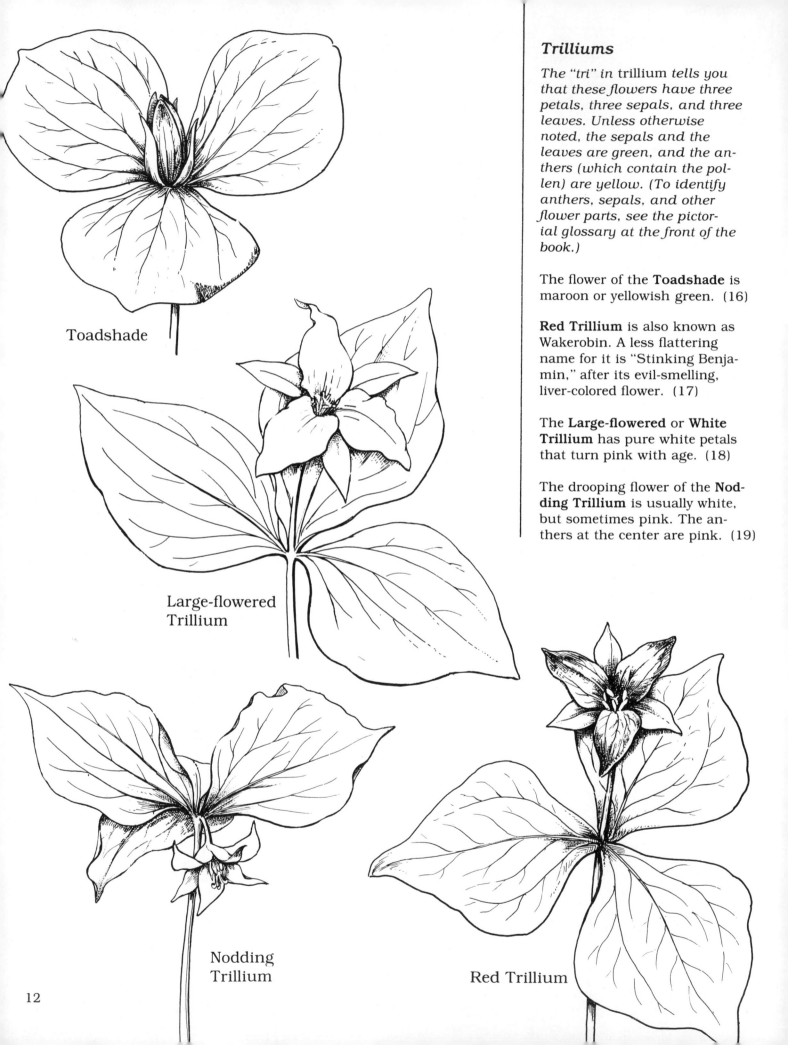

Toadshade

Large-flowered
Trillium

Nodding
Trillium

Red Trillium

Trilliums

The "tri" in trillium tells you that these flowers have three petals, three sepals, and three leaves. Unless otherwise noted, the sepals and the leaves are green, and the anthers (which contain the pollen) are yellow. (To identify anthers, sepals, and other flower parts, see the pictorial glossary at the front of the book.)

The flower of the **Toadshade** is maroon or yellowish green. (16)

Red Trillium is also known as Wakerobin. A less flattering name for it is "Stinking Benjamin," after its evil-smelling, liver-colored flower. (17)

The **Large-flowered** or **White Trillium** has pure white petals that turn pink with age. (18)

The drooping flower of the **Nodding Trillium** is usually white, but sometimes pink. The anthers at the center are pink. (19)

12

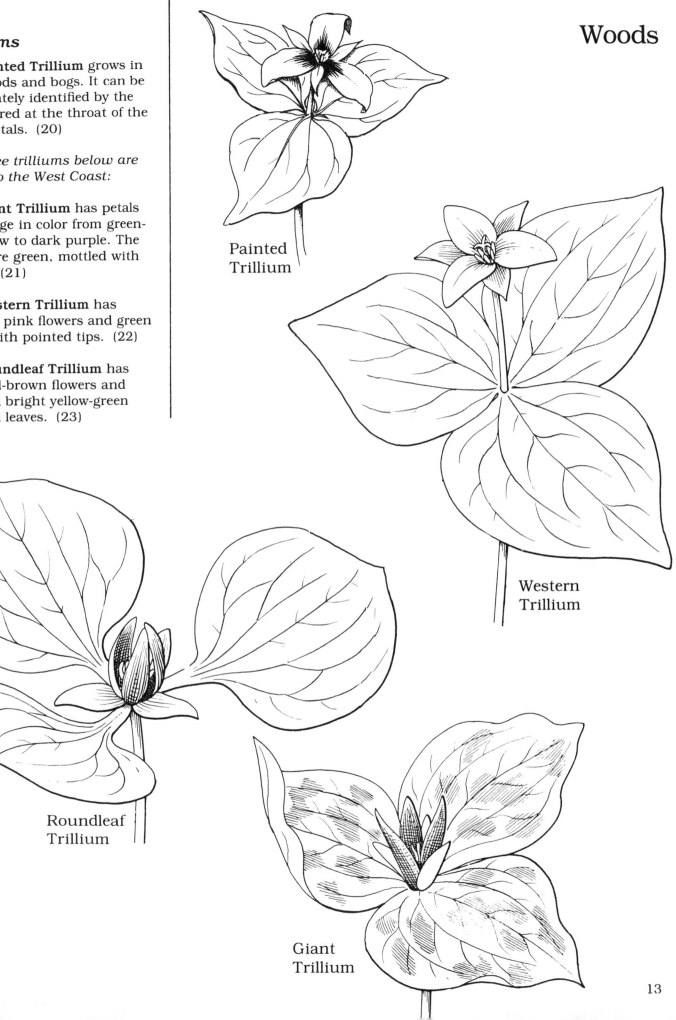

Trilliums

The **Painted Trillium** grows in acid woods and bogs. It can be immediately identified by the blaze of red at the throat of the white petals. (20)

The three trilliums below are native to the West Coast:

The **Giant Trillium** has petals that range in color from greenish yellow to dark purple. The leaves are green, mottled with purple. (21)

The **Western Trillium** has white to pink flowers and green leaves with pointed tips. (22)

The **Roundleaf Trillium** has dark red-brown flowers and rounded bright yellow-green rounded leaves. (23)

Painted
Trillium

Western
Trillium

Roundleaf
Trillium

Giant
Trillium

Woods

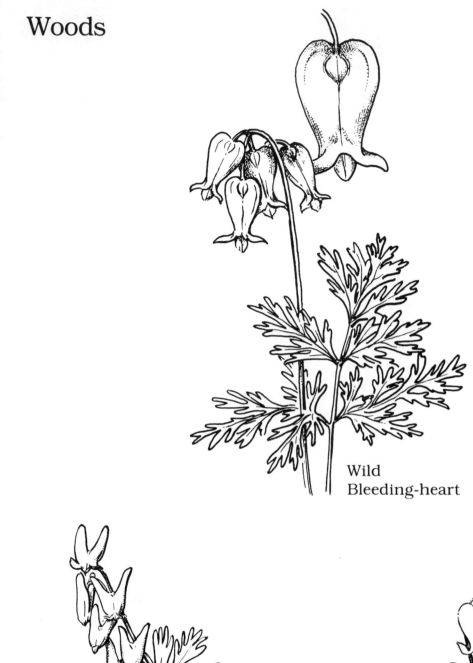

Wild
Bleeding-heart

Bleeding-hearts

The heart-shaped flowers of the **Wild Bleeding-heart,** dripping "drops of blood," vary in color from deep pink to reddish purple. (24)

The white flowers of **Dutchman's-breeches** look like tiny, upside-down pantaloons. Where the waist would be, each flower is tipped with yellow. (25)

The flowers of **Squirrel-corn** are greenish white and the leaves are gray-green. The name comes from the roots, which look like kernels of yellow corn. (26)

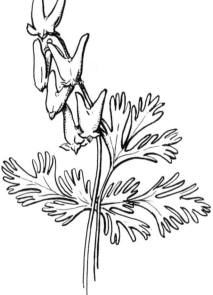

Dutchman's-breeches

Squirrel-corn

Bell-shaped Flowers

Pairs of yellow-green flowers hang like bells beneath the curved stem of **Great Solomon's-seal.** (27)

Mertensia is also called Virginia Cowslip or Virginia Bluebells. The pink buds open into blue flowers. (28)

Wintergreen has waxy white bells hanging beneath dark, shiny green leaves. The fragrant berry is red. See p. 17 for two other wintergreens. (29)

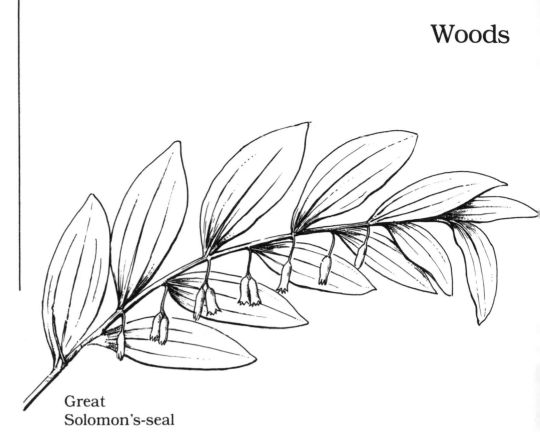

Great
Solomon's-seal

Mertensia

Wintergreen

Woods

Spring-beauty

Five-petaled Flowers

Spring-beauty has white or pink flowers with dark pink veins. The golden stamens end in pink anthers. (30)

The waxy white or pinkish petals of **Pipsissewa** surround a ring of reddish anthers. The undersides of the dark green leaves are reddish. (31)

The **Wild Geranium** is also called Cranesbill. If you look carefully, you'll see a sharp "beak" (the crane's bill) at the center of the rose-purple flower. (32)

Pipsissewa

Wild Geranium

16

Five-petaled Flowers

The **Pink Pyrola** belongs to the wintergreen family. The flowers are pink or crimson with a long protruding style at the center (see pictorial glossary). (33)

The single nodding flower of the **One-flowered Wintergreen** is waxy white or pink. The roundish leaves at the base of the stem are quite small. (34)

The **Common Blue Violet** grows in meadows as well as damp woods. The flower is violet with a white center. The three lower petals are strongly veined. (35)

One-flowered
Wintergreen

Pink Pyrola

Common
Blue Violet

Woods

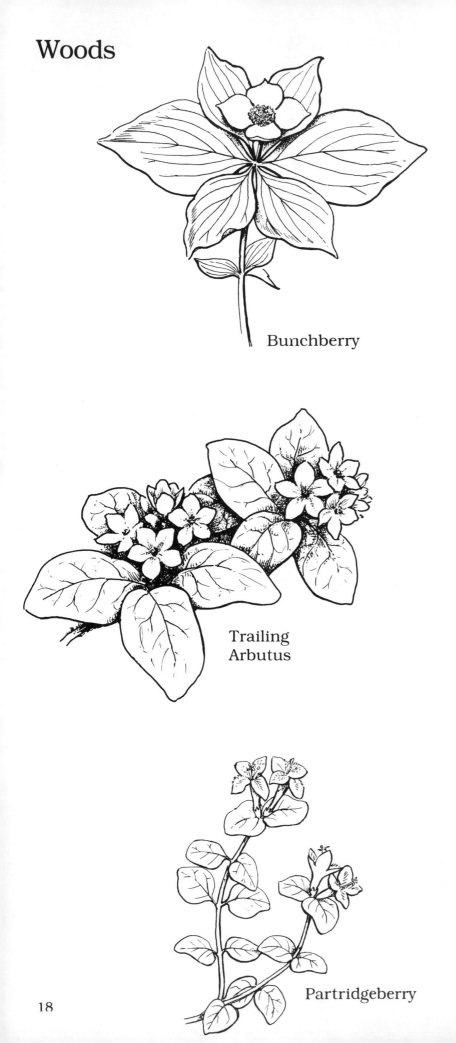

Bunchberry

Trailing
Arbutus

Partridgeberry

Bunchberry is a low-growing member of the dogwood family. The four white petals are actually bracts (modified leaves). They surround a cluster of tiny greenish flowers. The whorl of six leaves is dark green. (36)

Trailing Arbutus or **Mayflower**, the state flower of Massachusetts, is a flat creeping evergreen with leathery, green to bronze leaves and pink or white flowers. The flowers have a lovely scent (although you may have to put your face to the ground to smell it). (37)

A pair of pink or white flowers appears at the end of each creeping stem of the **Partridgeberry.** When the two flowers have finished blooming, a single red berry takes their place. (38)

The **Twinflower,** a dainty creeper, has a pair of small pink bells nodding at the top of a slender stem. The flowers are very fragrant. (39)

Twinflower

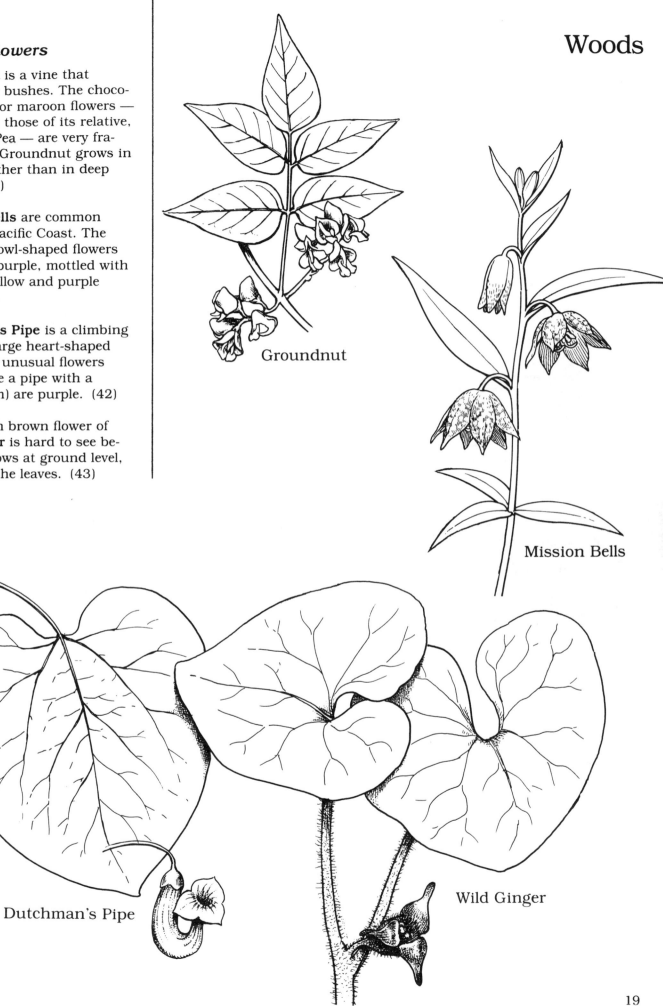

Woods

Brown Flowers

Groundnut is a vine that climbs over bushes. The chocolate brown or maroon flowers — shaped like those of its relative, the Sweet Pea — are very fragrant. The Groundnut grows in thickets rather than in deep woods. (40)

Mission Bells are common along the Pacific Coast. The nodding, bowl-shaped flowers are brown-purple, mottled with greenish yellow and purple spots. (41)

Dutchman's Pipe is a climbing vine with large heart-shaped leaves. The unusual flowers (shaped like a pipe with a curved stem) are purple. (42)

The reddish brown flower of **Wild Ginger** is hard to see because it grows at ground level, hidden by the leaves. (43)

Groundnut

Mission Bells

Dutchman's Pipe

Wild Ginger

19

Woods

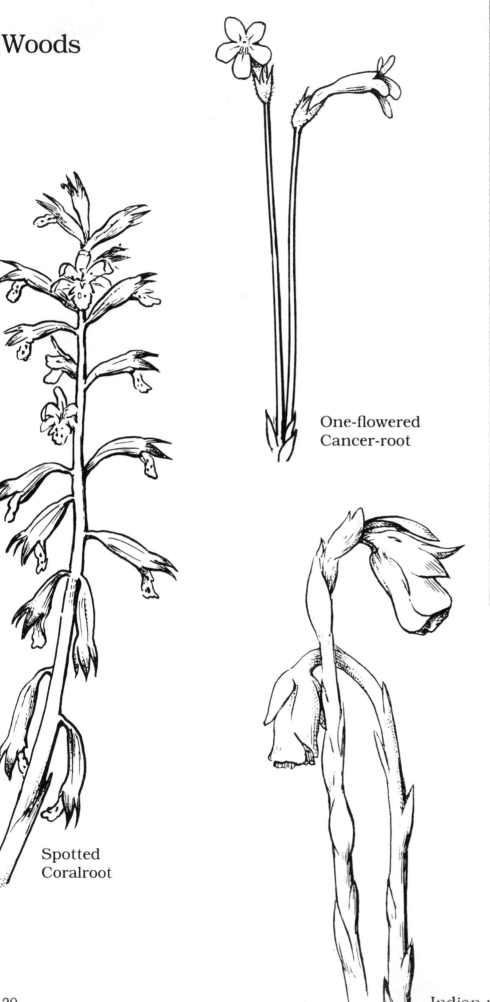

One-flowered
Cancer-root

Spotted
Coralroot

Indian-pipe

Parasitic Plants

These plants have no green pigment (chlorophyll) and therefore cannot manufacture their own food through photosynthesis. They live on roots or decaying plant material. They cannot be successfully transplanted and no one should try.

All parts of the **One-flowered Cancer-root** are brownish, except for the flower, which may be white or pale lavender with a yellow center. (44)

Indian-pipe is a ghostly plant with a thick white stem and one white or pink drooping flower. It grows in deep woods and turns black when it ages or is picked. (45)

Spotted Coralroot is a member of the orchid family. The stalk is yellowish or brownish. The flowers are tawny yellow, deepening to dull purple or purple-brown. The lower lip of each flower is white, spotted with red. Like other coralroots, this plant is actually a saprophyte, not a parasite, because it lives on decaying leaves instead of other plants. (46)

Parasitic Plants

Beechdrops have yellowish, reddish, or brown flowers on light brown stems. The plant lives under beech trees, where it gets nourishment from the roots. (47)

Similar in shape to the Indian-pipe, **Pinesap** has several nodding flowers instead of just one. The stem and flowers are the same color — tan, dull yellow, or reddish. This plant, another saprophyte, lives on leaf mold. (48)

The tawny or yellow-brown stalk of the **Squawroot** is scaly, suggesting a pine cone. The hooded, lipped flowers are also yellowish or light brown. This plant is parasitic on the roots of trees, especially oaks. (49)

Beechdrops

Pinesap

Squawroot

45

8

9

36

34

35

J. Savage

Woods Scene

27

18

43

33

17

32

Fields

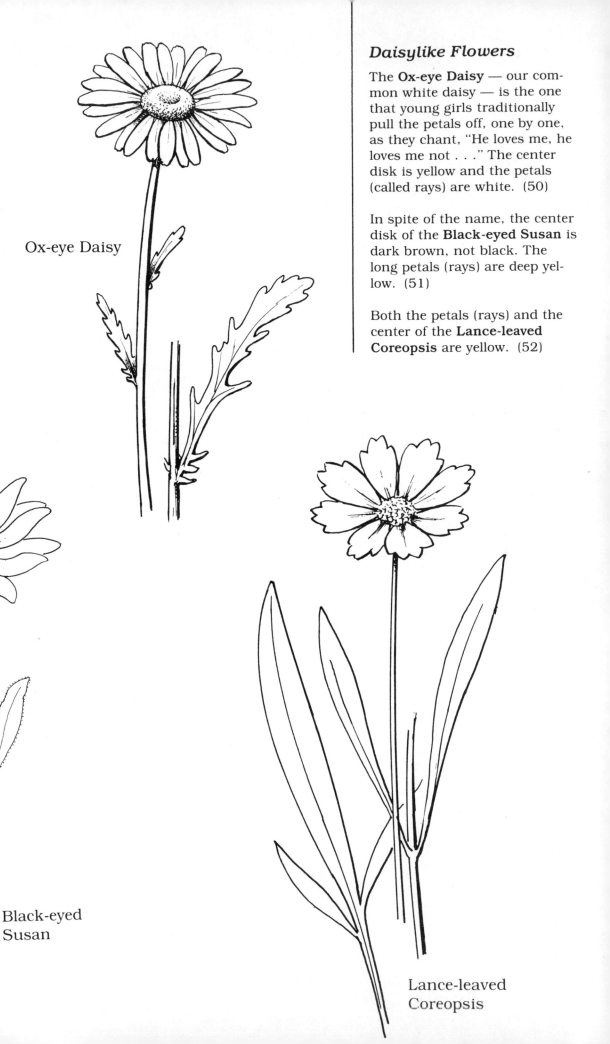

Ox-eye Daisy

Black-eyed
Susan

Lance-leaved
Coreopsis

Daisylike Flowers

The **Ox-eye Daisy** — our common white daisy — is the one that young girls traditionally pull the petals off, one by one, as they chant, "He loves me, he loves me not . . ." The center disk is yellow and the petals (called rays) are white. (50)

In spite of the name, the center disk of the **Black-eyed Susan** is dark brown, not black. The long petals (rays) are deep yellow. (51)

Both the petals (rays) and the center of the **Lance-leaved Coreopsis** are yellow. (52)

Lilies

The petals of the **Turk's-cap Lily** curve back, suggesting a rounded fez, or "Turk's cap." Shade them from dark orange at the outside to yellow with a green star in the center. The stamens are very long and yellow, with brown anthers at the tips. This lily grows in wet meadows as well as in dry fields. (53)

Like the Turk's-cap (above), the **Canada Lily** also grows in wet meadows. The bell-shaped flowers are usually yellow or orange, sometimes red. (54)

In spite of its name, the **Wood Lily** usually grows in the open. This orange to scarlet lily is the only *spotted* lily that blooms face up. Day-lilies (which are not true lilies, anyway) hold their blossoms up, but they are not spotted. (55)

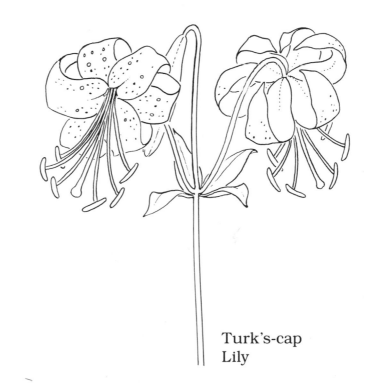

Turk's-cap Lily

Canada Lily

Wood Lily

Fields

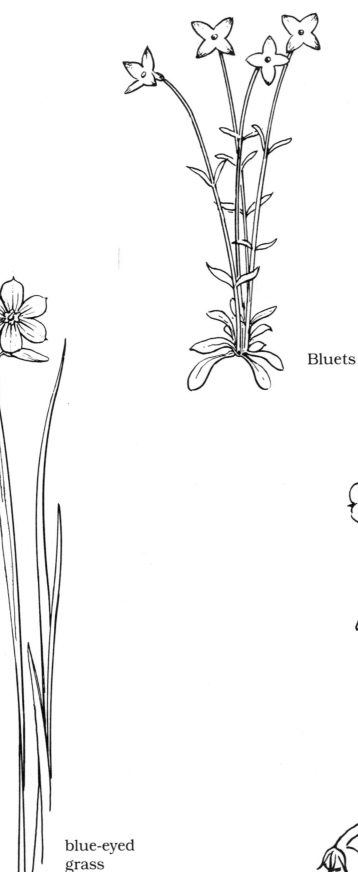

Bluets

Tiny Treasures

Bluets are also called Quaker Ladies or Innocence. The stamens in the center are yellow. The petals are light blue with a white ring near the center. (56)

The **Scarlet Pimpernel** usually has scarlet flowers, although they may be blue or white. The flowers close up in cloudy weather. (57)

The **blue-eyed grasses** have irislike leaves, with tiny flowers ("eyes") at the tips. The flowers are usually deep blue-violet with a yellow center. (58)

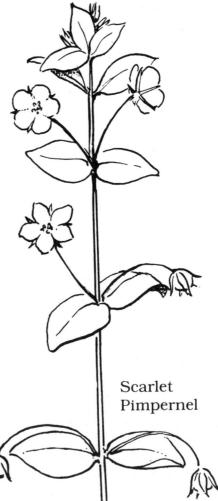

Scarlet
Pimpernel

blue-eyed
grass

Morning and Evening Flowers

The delicate light blue flowers of the **Flax** plant open in the morning and close by afternoon. (59)

The brilliant blue flowers of the **Chicory** open in the morning and start to close by noon. (60)

The yellow flowers of the **Common Evening-primrose** open toward evening and wilt the next day. Since one flower opens at a time, the plant may bloom for days or even weeks. (61)

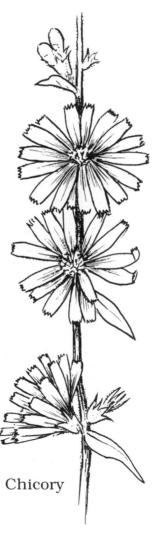

Flax

Chicory

Common
Evening-primrose

27

Fields

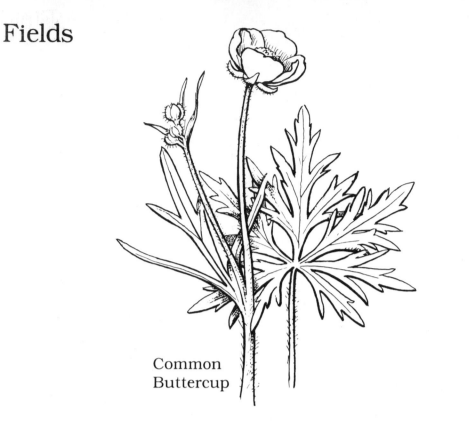

Common
Buttercup

Of the dozens of buttercups, the **Common Buttercup** is the most familiar. If you hold the flower under your chin and the pollen comes off on your skin, it means you like butter. The leaves are deeply notched and the flower is a deep, glossy yellow. (62)

The **Common Tansy** is a tall straight plant topped with many yellow buttons — like tiny daisies without the petals. The fernlike leaves are bright green. (63)

Curled Dock, a tall coarse plant, is popular in dried flower arrangements. The flowers start out green, turn rosy pink (a good time to pick them), and then dark brown. (64)

Curled Dock

Common
Tansy

Roadside Plants

Viper's Bugloss is a bristly, odd-looking plant with bright blue flowers. The upper lip of the flower is longer than the lower one, and the red stamens project beyond both lips. The name probably refers to the fact that the plant was once used as a remedy for snakebite. (65)

The flowers of the **Common St. Johnswort** are bright yellow, with bushy yellow stamens in the center. The tiny dots along the edges of the petals are almost black. (66)

Although the flowers look rather ragged when examined up close, **Bouncing Bet** makes attractive colonies along roadsides and railroad banks. The flowers are magenta, pink, or white. (67)

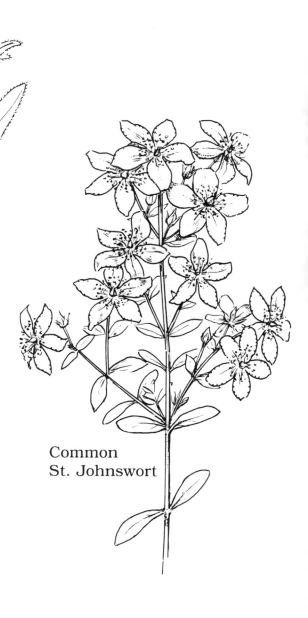

Viper's Bugloss

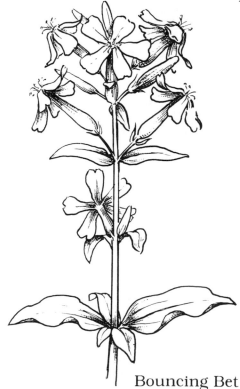

Bouncing Bet

Common St. Johnswort

Fields

Although it looks like a smaller version of the western desert plant, the **Yucca,** or Spanish Bayonet, actually grows along the Atlantic coastal plain, in sterile sandy soil. The very tall stem rises from a rosette of stiff, spiky leaves, each about 2½ feet long. The flowers are greenish white. (68)

A coarse, bushy plant, **Pokeweed** grows from 4 to 10 feet tall. The stem is reddish, the flowers are greenish white, and the berries (which can be used to make a dye) are purple-black. (69)

Yucca

Pokeweed

Large Roadside Plants

The **Common Mullein,** a large plant of roadsides and fields, grows from 2 to 6 feet tall. The leaves, which feel like soft flannel, are a light gray-green. The yellow flowers on the clublike head open gradually. (70)

The **Common Sunflower** may grow as tall as 12 feet (but is usually shorter). It has a large brown disk surrounded by yellow petals (rays). (71)

The flower head of the **Teasel** looks like an oval pincushion, with its dense cluster of tiny lavender florets and spines. It makes an interesting dried flower if you don't mind working with the prickly stem. (72)

Common Mullein

Teasel

Common Sunflower

Fields

Everlasting
Pea

Pea-like Flowers

The flowers on these two pages belong to the pea family, which also includes peas, beans, and clovers. The flowers in the group shown here have a typical shape, which is probably best known from the Sweet Pea.

The **Everlasting Pea** — a very large sweet pea (without the scent) — comes in pink, blue, or white. It grows like a vine, tumbling over other plants. (73)

Broom is a bush with tiny gray-green leaves and yellow flowers. Note the pod with its "peas" inside. (74)

Broom

32

Pea-like Flowers

Wild Indigo is a small bushy plant with yellow flowers and gray-green stems and leaves. The leaves turn black when dried. (75)

Wild Lupine is light blue and smaller than the cultivated lupine, which is sometimes found growing in the wild as an "escape" from gardens. (76)

The flowers of **Crown-vetch**, a groundcover, are bicolored — pink and white. (77)

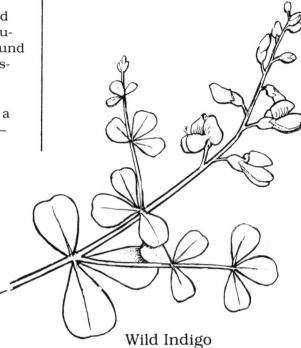

Wild Indigo

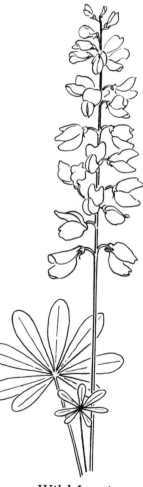

Wild Lupine

Crown-vetch

Fields

Note the unique flower structure and the long, pointed seedpod of the **Common Milkweed.** The seeds are attached to white wings (like those of a dandelion) inside the pod, which is gray-green. The flowers of this milkweed tend to droop. They come in shades of dusty rose, lavender, and dull brownish purple. (78)

The bright orange flowers of the **Butterfly-weed** make this the handsomest milkweed and attract lots of butterflies. This plant is sometimes called "pleurisy root" because the Indians supposedly chewed the root as a cure for chest ailments. (79)

Common
Milkweed

Butterfly-weed

34

Look-alikes

Steeplebush's spire of fuzzy, dusty rose flowers blooms from the top down. The undersides of the leaves are light brown and woolly. The plant is found in low wet areas as well as in fields. (80)

The pale pink or white flowers of **Meadowsweet** grow in a wider, looser cluster than the flowers of the Steeplebush. The stems are reddish or brownish, and the undersides of the leaves are green and not woolly. (81)

Steeplebush

Meadowsweet

Fields

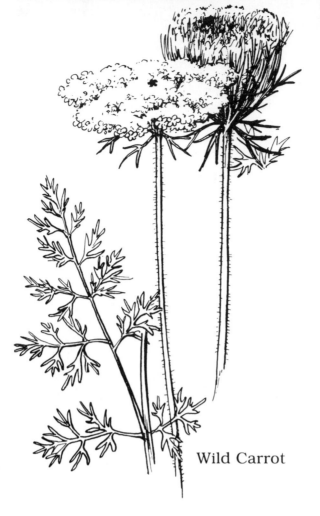

Wild Carrot

Look-alikes

The **Wild Carrot** is better known as Queen Anne's Lace. A tiny purple-black floret is often present at the center of the cluster of tiny white flowers. Old flower clusters curl up into a tan-colored "bird's nest." (82)

Poison Hemlock's white flowers grow in a rounder, looser cluster, and do not have the dark center floret of the Wild Carrot (Queen Anne's Lace). Unlike the Wild Carrot, Poison Hemlock is very poisonous. (83)

Although it is often confused with the other plants on this page because of its clusters of white flowers, **Boneset** is really quite different. The flowers are fuzzier and the leaves are distinctive in shape and arrangement. (84)

The clustered flowers of the **Yarrow** (see facing page) are generally dull white, but are occasionally pink or yellow. The foliage is grayish green. (85)

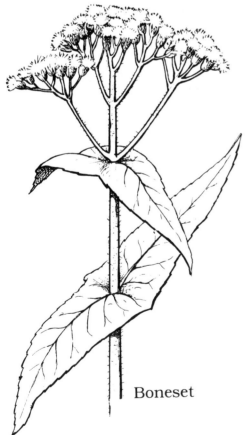

Boneset

Poison Hemlock

36

Other Flowers in Clusters

Feverfew, a wild chrysanthemum, has short, white, daisy-like petals surrounding a relatively large yellow button. (86)

The little flowers of **Pearly Everlasting** have protruding yellow centers surrounded by dry white petals (bracts). The foliage is gray-green on top, whitish green below. (87)

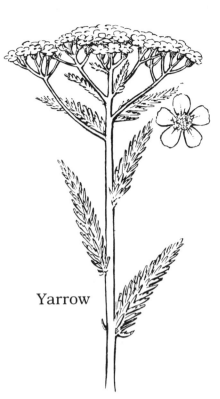

Yarrow

Feverfew

Pearly Everlasting

Fields

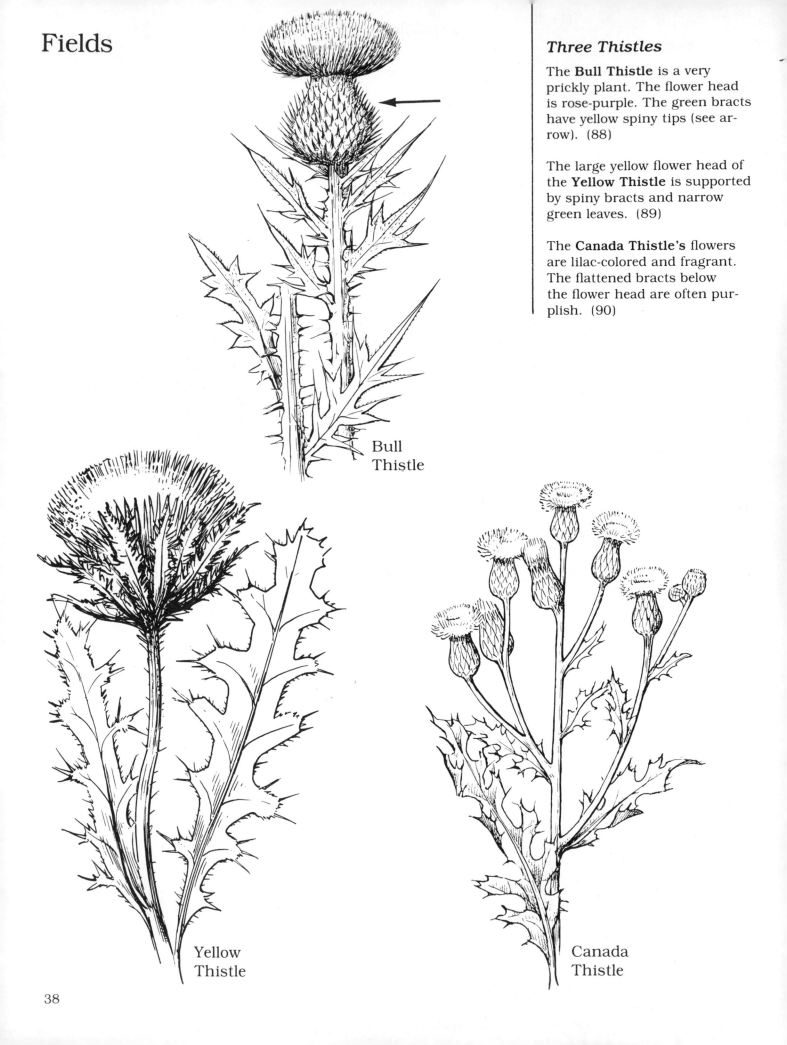

Bull Thistle

Yellow Thistle

Canada Thistle

Three Thistles

The **Bull Thistle** is a very prickly plant. The flower head is rose-purple. The green bracts have yellow spiny tips (see arrow). (88)

The large yellow flower head of the **Yellow Thistle** is supported by spiny bracts and narrow green leaves. (89)

The **Canada Thistle's** flowers are lilac-colored and fragrant. The flattened bracts below the flower head are often purplish. (90)

Prairie Flowers

The reddish purple petals (rays) of the **Purple Coneflower** curve downward from the high, tufted center cone, which is also reddish purple. (91) The **Green-headed Coneflower** (not shown), which also grows on the prairies, has yellow petals and a greenish cone or disk.

The **Pasqueflower** varies in color from blue to purple to white, with many yellow stamens and pistils in the center. The leaves and stems are covered with silky hairs. (92)

The **Painted-cup** is also known as Indian Paintbrush. There are several kinds of paintbrushes, which are recognizable by their brilliant scarlet-tipped bracts. In this species, the lower part of the bract is light green, and the real flower, which you will notice after you color in the bracts, is greenish yellow with a protruding pistil. (93)

The beardtongues, or penstemons, are another large group of plants, often hard to tell apart. They get their name from the tufted stamen (the "bearded tongue") in the throat of the flower. This species, the **Large-flowered Beardtongue**, has pale lavender-blue or violet flowers. The leaves are a pale bluish green. (94)

Purple
Coneflower

Painted-cup

Pasqueflower

Large-flowered
Beardtongue

39

Fields

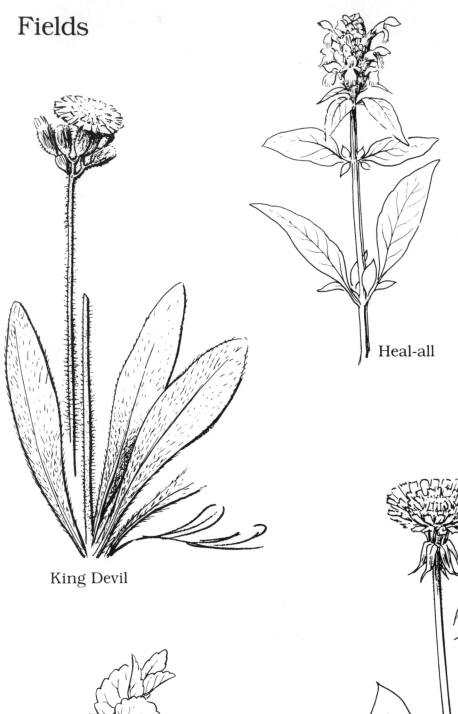

King Devil

Heal-all

King Devil is a hairy yellow hawkweed, similar to the Orange Hawkweed or Devil's Paintbrush. (95)

Gill-over-the-Ground is also called Ground Ivy. A real lawn pest, but a rather pretty one, it forms mats of scalloped green to purplish leaves and violet flowers. (96)

Heal-all is also called Selfheal because it used to be made into an herbal medicine. The violet flowers are hooded, with a fringed lower lip. (97)

If the **Common Dandelion** didn't take over the lawn, it would have as many admirers as other wildflowers do. The flower at the left is bright yellow. The one at the right is past its prime — about to balloon into a fluffy white seedhead. (98)

Gill-over-the-Ground

Common Dandelion

Vacant-lot Plants

The showy **Fireweed** is one of the first plants to spring up after a fire. The stamens have yellow filaments and brownish anthers. The seedpods point upward between the leaves and the flowers and turn reddish when they are ripe. (99)

Lady's-thumb belongs to a group called smartweeds. The tight cluster of flowers is dusty pink and the stems are reddish. Note the fringed sheath on the stem (see arrow in close-up). The leaves are green with darker green splotches. (100)

The snapdragonlike flowers of **Butter-and-Eggs** have orange "tongues" between the upper and lower yellow lips. When a bee lands on the orange part, the flower opens up and the bee enters to gather the pollen. (101)

Fireweed

Lady's-thumb

Butter-and-Eggs

Fields

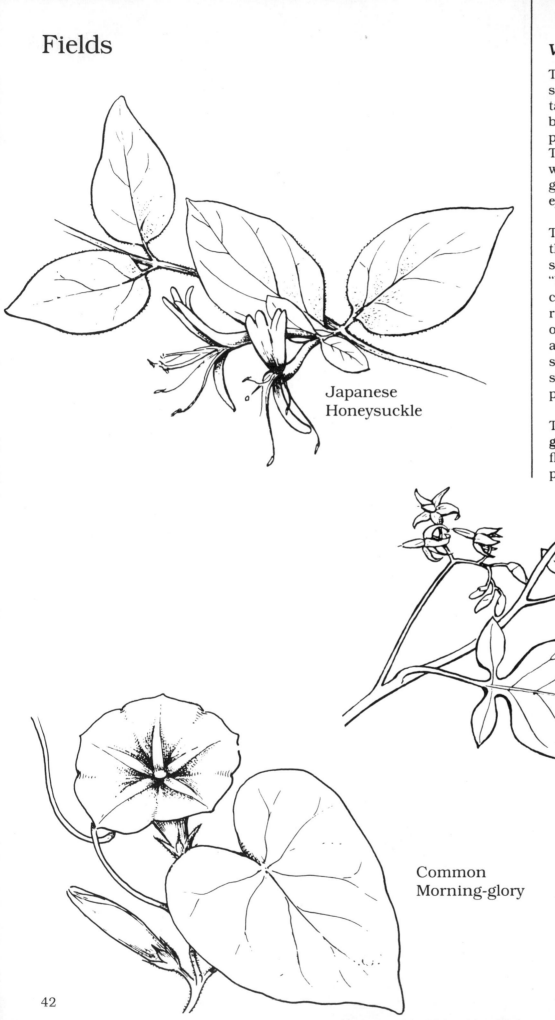

Japanese
Honeysuckle

Nightshade

Common
Morning-glory

Vines

The **Japanese Honeysuckle** is such a weedy vine that it can take over entire embankments, but few "weeds" have such pretty, sweet-smelling flowers! The flowers are yellow and white, and the leaves are dark green. The berries of this honeysuckle are black. (102)

The five swept-back petals of the **Nightshade** are violet (or sometimes white), with a yellow "beak" protruding from the center of each flower. The berries are bright red and appear on the vine while the flowers are still blooming. This plant is sometimes called "Deadly Nightshade" because the berries are poisonous. (103)

This is the **Common Morning-glory,** a well-known garden flower. Color it blue, white, purple, or pink. (104)

Late Summer Flowers

There are about six dozen varieties of **goldenrod** that come in five different shapes (see below). In all cases, as the name tells us, the flowers are golden yellow. (105)

The **New England Aster** is the showiest of the many different asters. The flowers have deep violet petals surrounding a golden center. (106)

Goldenrod

New England
Aster

*plumelike,
graceful*   *elm-
branched*   *clublike,
showy*   *wandlike,
slender*   *flat-
topped*

60

104

82

67

50

62

98

V. Savage

70

71

79

63

51

101

Wetlands

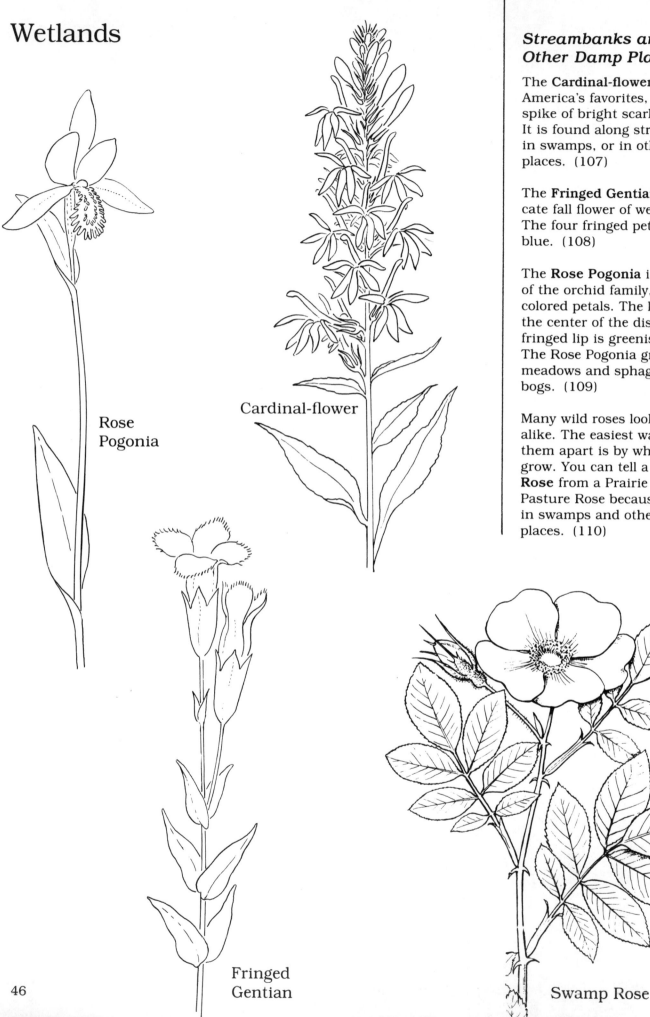

Rose
Pogonia

Cardinal-flower

Fringed
Gentian

Swamp Rose

Streambanks and Other Damp Places

The **Cardinal-flower,** one of America's favorites, is a slender spike of bright scarlet flowers. It is found along streambanks, in swamps, or in other wet places. (107)

The **Fringed Gentian** is a delicate fall flower of wet meadows. The four fringed petals are deep blue. (108)

The **Rose Pogonia** is a member of the orchid family, with rose-colored petals. The line down the center of the distinctive fringed lip is greenish yellow. The Rose Pogonia grows in wet meadows and sphagnum bogs. (109)

Many wild roses look very much alike. The easiest way to tell them apart is by where they grow. You can tell a **Swamp Rose** from a Prairie Rose or a Pasture Rose because it grows in swamps and other wet places. (110)

Wild Relatives of Garden Flowers

The upright petals of the **Larger Blue Flag** are violet. The three lower ones have a touch of yellow at the throat, a large patch of white in the center, and a wide band of purple around the edge. The petals of this wild iris are veined with purple. (111)

The flowers of the **True Forget-me-not** are sky blue with a yellow eye. Some forget-me-nots are native to North America but this kind was originally imported from Europe as a garden flower. (112)

The **Swamp Rose-mallow** is a tall plant with a large, clear pink flower that looks like a hollyhock (both plants belong to the mallow family). The reproductive organs (stamens and pistils) in the center are yellow. The leaves are light green. (113)

Larger
Blue Flag

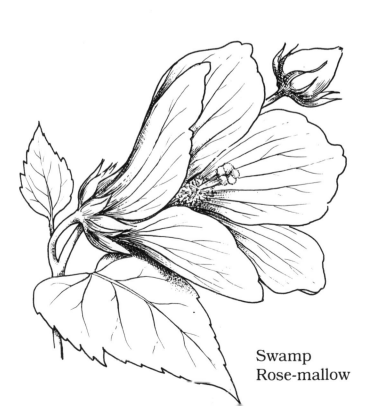

Swamp
Rose-mallow

True
Forget-me-not

47

Wetlands

Yellow
Loosestrife

Swamp Candles and Other Spires

The yellow starlike flowers of the **Yellow Loosestrife** have circles of red spots on the petals. Masses of these "swamp candles" brighten up a patch of wetland. (114)

The tall spiked flowers of the **Purple Loosestrife** often carpet swampy meadows with magenta. (115)

The tufted flower heads of the **Dense Blazing-star** are rose-purple. The scaly bracts that support the flowers are purple or green with purple edges. (116)

Dense
Blazing-star

Purple
Loosestrife

Tubed and Lipped Flowers

If you touch the **Spotted Touch-me-not** when its seeds are ripe, the seedpod will pop open. This plant is also called Jewelweed because the orange blossom hangs like a jeweled pendant. (117)

The **Purple Gerardia** is the largest of the many gerardias, although the flowers are only an inch long. The purple flowers look like inflated tubes or trumpets. (118)

The flowers of the **Mad-dog Skullcap** are usually violet or blue. The square stem identifies it as a member of the mint family. Most of the skullcaps have ordinary names like "downy," "hairy," or "showy." Where do you think this name came from? (119)

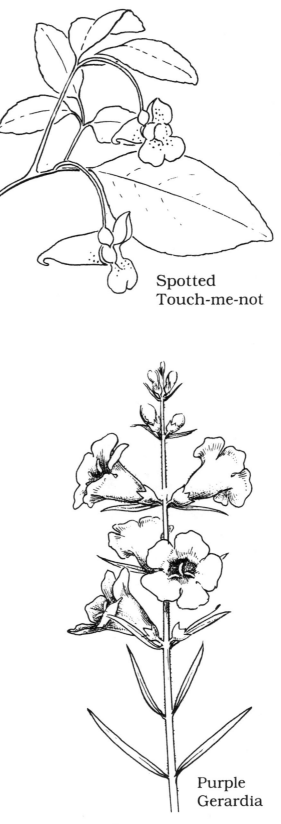

Spotted
Touch-me-not

Purple
Gerardia

Mad-dog
Skullcap

Wetlands

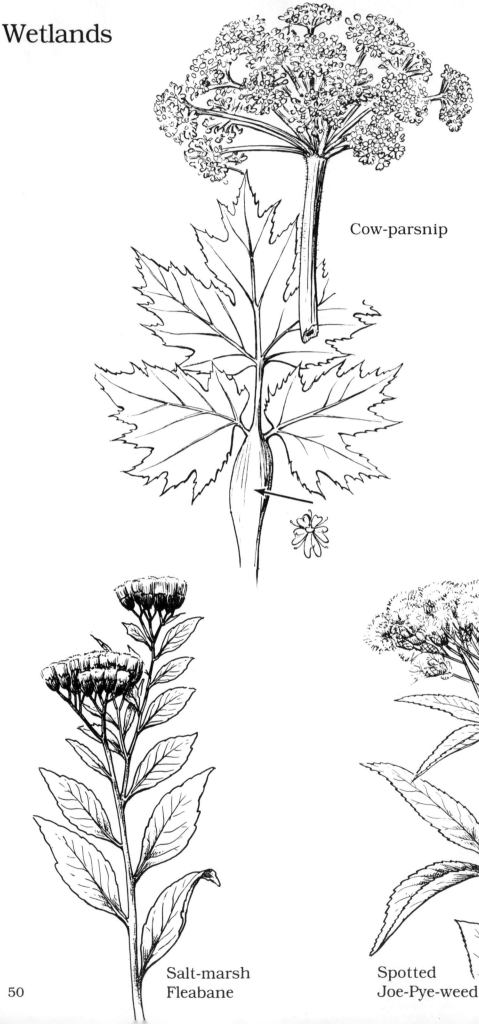

Cow-parsnip

Salt-marsh
Fleabane

Spotted
Joe-Pye-weed

Flowers in Clusters

The **Cow-parsnip** is a huge, woolly, evil-smelling plant. Its whitish flowers (tinged with purple) grow in a round cluster similar to the flowers of wild carrots, parsleys, parsnips, hemlocks, caraways, and other related plants. This plant grows up to 10 feet tall. Its leaves grow out of an inflated sheath on the stem (see arrow in close-up). (120)

The sticky, camphor-smelling **Salt-marsh Fleabane** has pink-purple flowers. In earlier times, the flowers were dried and used to keep fleas out of the house. (121)

Joe-Pye-weeds are large plants topped with dusty purple flower heads. The **Spotted Joe-Pye-weed** has a stem that is purple or spotted with purple. (122)

Hooded Flowers

The flaplike spathe (the "pulpit") of **Jack-in-the-Pulpit** is green or purplish brown, and almost always striped. It forms a canopy over the flower stalk (the "Jack"), which is green or purple. (123)

The mottled spathe of **Skunk Cabbage** varies from green to purple-brown, and almost covers the rounded yellow flower stalk. The green leaves, which emerge after the flower is up, are the source of the unpleasant odor. (124)

The slender spadix (flower stalk) of the **Arrow Arum,** with its greenish flowers, is almost covered by the long greenish spathe that wraps around it. (125)

Jack-in-the-Pulpit

Arrow Arum

Skunk Cabbage

Wetlands

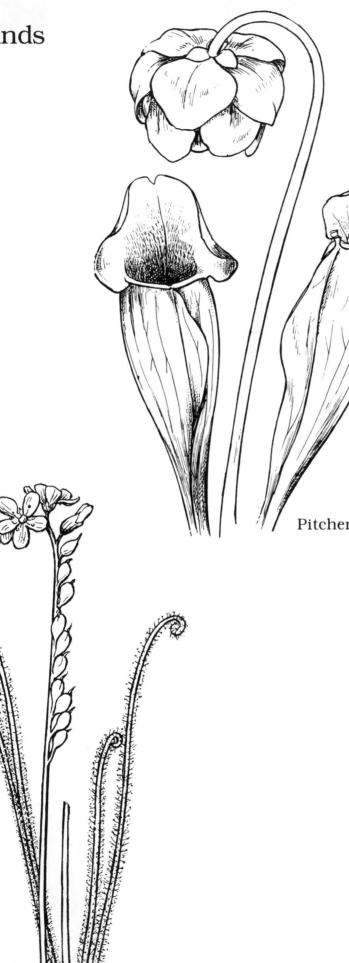

Pitcher-plant

Insect-eating Plants

The **Pitcher-plant** is a native of bogs, with a dull red flower. The leaves (the "pitchers") are red or green with heavy veins. The bristles near the top trap insects, which drop into the water in the pitcher. (126)

The **Round-leaved Sundew**, another insect-eater, traps its prey in a different manner. Insects are caught in a sticky juice that oozes from the reddish hairs on the green leaves. The pink or white flowers open one at a time. This sundew grows in acid or peaty bogs. (127)

The **Thread-leaved Sundew** grows in damp sand along the coast in the Northeast. In this sundew the sticky hairs are on upright leaves. The flowers are purple. (128)

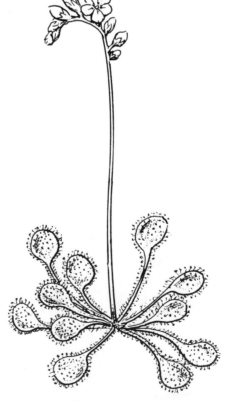

Thread-leaved
Sundew

Round-leaved
Sundew

Shallow-water Plants

These flowers grow in ditches, swamps, and marshes.

There are dozens of smart-weeds. Notice the similarities between this one — the **Water Smartweed** — and the Lady's Thumb on p. 41, which is a relative. The flower cluster of the Water Smartweed is also dusty pink. (129)

Sea-lavender is a salt-marsh plant of late summer, when it casts a lavender haze over the marshes. When the tide is low, you can pick this plant. It will keep indefinitely, although the lavender flowers will lose much of their color. The leaves are dark green to bronze. (130)

The **Golden Club** has a cluster of tiny bright yellow flowers at the end of a long, golden, club-like spadix (flower stalk). The leaves are dark green. (131)

Water Smartweed

Sea-lavender

Golden Club

Wetlands

Common
Cattail

Shallow-water Plants

The **Common Cattail** is a tall plant that grows in dense clumps. The dark brown, sausage-shaped flower head is made up of tiny, closely packed female flowers. The more slender "tail" that extends above the flower head contains the lighter tan male flowers. (132)

The leaves of the **Water-willow** are light green. The flowers are bicolored — pale violet or white, with purple spots. (133)

Water-willow

Water Plants

The blue spires of the **Pickerel-weed** form beds in shallow water at the edges of ponds and streams. (134)

The green leaves of the **Fragrant Water-lily** have purple undersides and are like large platters. The white flowers are from 3 to 5 inches across and are very fragrant, as the name suggests. (135)

The bowl-shaped leaves of the **American Lotus** are dark green above and brownish green below. They can be as large as 2 feet across. The large yellow flower with an orange-yellow center blooms a foot or two above the water. (136)

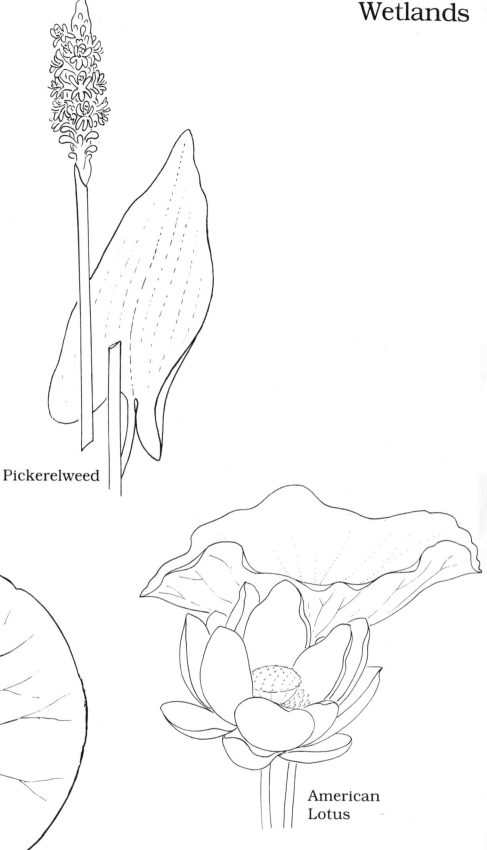

Pickerelweed

Fragrant
Water-lily

American
Lotus

113

111

107

111

53

V. Savage

Wetlands Scene

122

115

134

114

110

113

Sandy Soil

Beavertail
Cactus

Claret-cup
Cactus

Cacti

The pads of the **Beavertail Cactus,** which resemble the tail of a beaver, are blue. The flowers are red-purple. This is a common cactus of the Mojave and Colorado deserts. (137)

The yellowish green stems of the **Claret-cup Cactus** grow in low spreading mounds on dry mountain slopes. The flowers are scarlet-orange. (138)

Cacti

The **Red Barrel Cactus** is a single, large, barrel-shaped cactus that is 1 to 5 feet tall. Each rib is covered with red spines, which give the whole cactus a reddish look. The flowers, on the other hand, are yellow. This cactus grows in the Mojave and Colorado deserts. (139)

The **Prickly-pear** is the only cactus that commonly grows in the eastern United States. The jointed pads are green. The showy yellow flower often has a red center. (140)

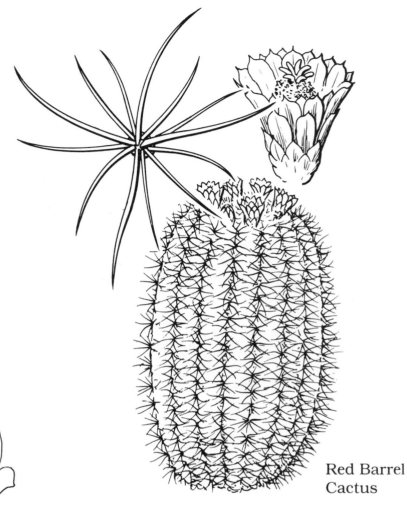

Red Barrel
Cactus

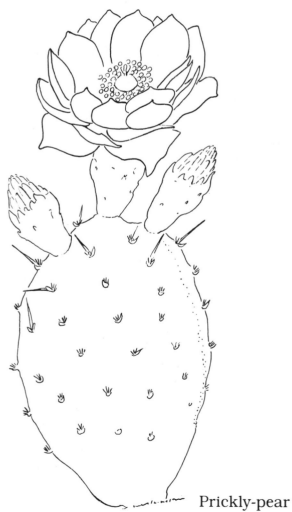

Prickly-pear

Sandy Soil

Rugosa Rose

Dune Plants

The story goes that the **Rugosa Rose,** an Asiatic plant, arrived in New England by way of a Japanese ship that was wrecked off the coast of Cape Cod. It is also known as the Wrinkled Rose or Beach Rose. The flowers are deep rose-pink or white, and the leaves are very wrinkled and dark green. (141)

The **Horn-poppy** is also called the Sea-poppy. The flowers are light yellow and the leaves are a very light gray-green. The long, sickle-shaped seedpod turns from pale tan to brown as the seeds ripen. (142)

The scaly gray-green foliage of **False Heather,** a low shrubby plant, reminds one of heather, which accounts for the name. The tiny flowers, which bloom briefly in June, are yellow. (143)

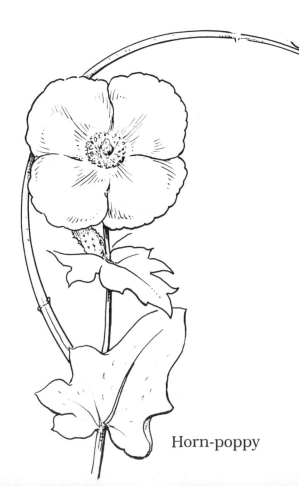

False Heather

Horn-poppy

Dune Plants

The **Beach Pea** has showy purple flowers. See pp. 32–33 for other members of the pea family. (144)

At the beach, this species of **Dusty Miller** makes great mounds of light gray-green leaves that have a whitish cast. The flower, which is not as attractive as the leaves, is dull yellow. (145)

Golden-asters are not true asters, but they also bloom late in the summer. This species, the **Sickle-leaved Golden-aster,** has stiff gray-green leaves and white woolly stems. The flowers are yellow. (146)

Sandy Soil

Beach Pea

Dusty Miller

Sickle-leaved Golden-aster

142

V. Savage

145

141

146

144

Sandy Soil Scene

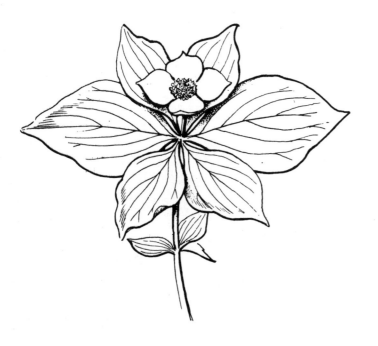

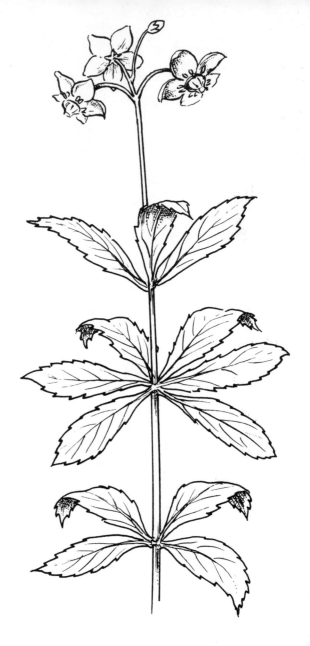

See if you can identify
these wildflowers.

64

70
71
72
73
74
75
76
77
78
79
80
81
82
83
84
85
86
87
88
89
90
91
92
93
94
95
96
97
98

Numbers are keyed to captions throughout the book.

99 100 101 102 103 104 105 106 107 108 109 110 111 112 113 114 115 116 117 118 119 120 121 122 123 124 125 126 127 128

Numbers are keyed to captions throughout the book.